SOMETHING WITH FEATHERS

Kati Mohr

AF280890

Kati Mohr

SOMETHING WITH FEATHERS

Tanka

Bibliographic information of the German National Library: The German National Library lists this publication in the German National Bibliography; detailed bibliographic data is available on the internet at http://dnb.dnb.de.

Proofreading:
Kati Mohr

Production & publisher:
BoD - Books on Demand, Norderstedt

ISBN: 978-3-7583-0668-6

when I came home
the world got wider

To Ken Slaughter

thank you
for having taught me
five lines
the outstretched fingers
of an open hand

TABLE OF CONTENT

MY FISTS CLENCHED

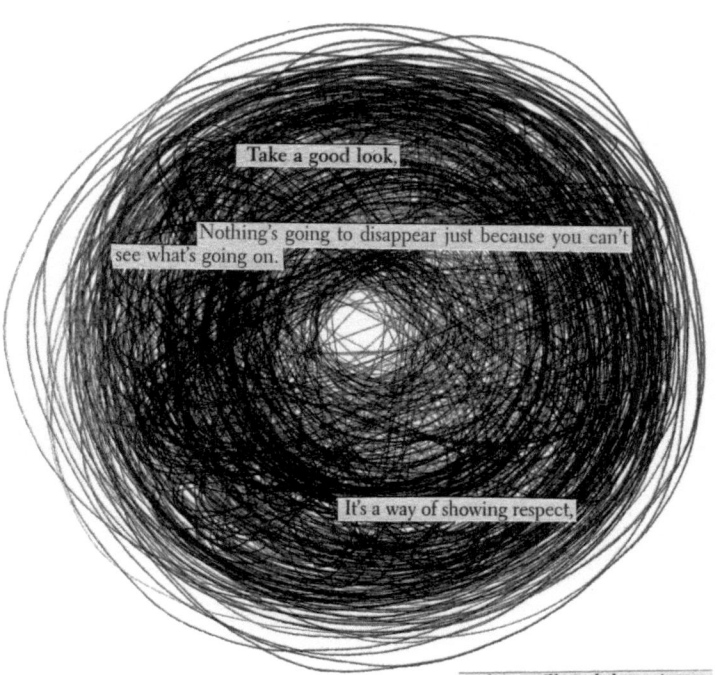

Take a good look,

Nothing's going to disappear just because you can't see what's going on.

It's a way of showing respect,

so large it'll rival the universe.

in the spitting rain
the flags just barely flutter;
I walk faster
with my fists clenched
till despair crawls in

snow can burn
it has a million ways of being
and melting
the way my eyes could
if

at night
my arms will hold
my chest
a shield against
what's tucked inside

if just
my heart quit
fluttering
along the trails
—running hares

dreams
of pulling all
too close
I wake up
even tighter

even as
a poppy bud
so ruffled
why is mama
surging in my head

earthgazing
for a little while
it seems
there are no wars
there are no walls

the garden path
so smooth
and yet
my head will scold the heart
for slipping

searching something
among ripe barley
just after dusk
words shouted from afar
the source of misunderstandings

shimmering
from a crimson leaf
last night's rain
settles
in my mind

kites in trees
the trades we do
in shame
coming
to a stillness

in a dim kitchen
waiting for the black ice
to happen
brimful
from these uneventful days

the magpie spreads
its feathers wide
apart
I ask my friend
who can I trust

BOWLS OF BLUE

depressed.

'But why? What happened?'

'Don' make me say it again.

a shadow
adrift on the water
in the end
what do you feel
what do I feel

something
under my nails
needs
the question
if I'm masking

on the hills
the hay bales
passing
I gather what
I can't remember

bowls of blue my whole life marbles thin as tea

over and over
I alter my position
in the pillows
full of hope
my past sinks in

the moon
unchanging
phases
the illusion
that I see myself

we are
the sum of our parts
at times
a crackle of wipers
dearly wanting to move

the arc of hands
that pause before they stir
the strings
yet if not touched
how could I resonate

rain
trickling down
the roof-light
say, what more
am I

sunflowers
pointing out
a blinding sun
I'll never know myself
completely

AGAIN I SEEK

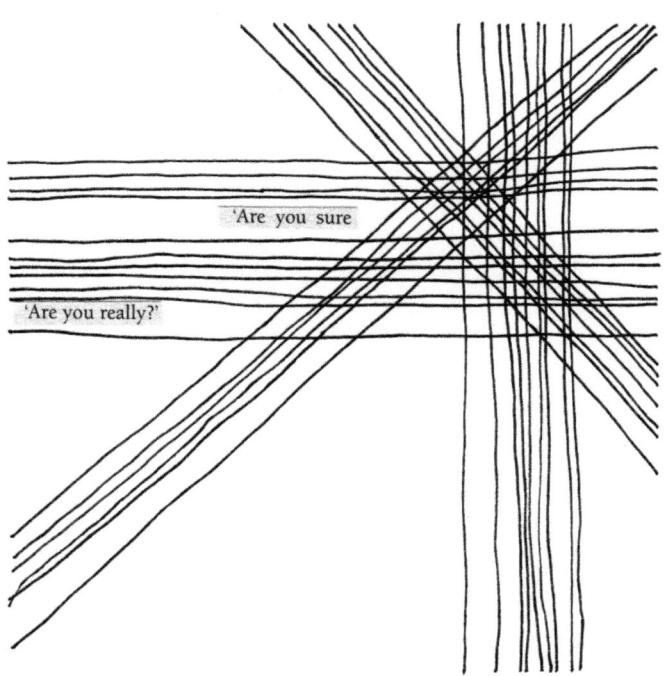

'Are you sure

'Are you really?'

an ache:
my life shall be
a season
unlike any
other

out at sea
a narrow silver line
lights up ...
and I at least want to remember
as if weighing it

death poems
till the night comes to a close
I understand
this craving for a coffee
when the day begins

again i seek
the presence of a tree
a comfort
as it can be touched
it can be climbed

my breaths
run through the arms of
a larch
almost alive
so am I

reaping
line after line
mirages
I keep holding fast
my clammy hands

I lie down
resting by my head
the sound of the river
a prayer
never a promise

the skin
of an apple
in my hand
as even as being
still upon the tree

just someone
to be found
in years to come
that makes me feel
okay

soft rain
upon the porch:
the change
I really need
in that tender way

the yellow leaves
flat on concrete
shine back at me
the seating angle
of my thoughts

WALKING HOME

all the words stowed deep in my heart,
a lunatic river. think about all the things I haven't said
"Holy shit,"
tucked so snug
an assortment of my worldly possessions.
can barely mask I've yet to crack the code."
It's clear
go outside to gather some sweet soft
the world's most badass work of art.
here for the ritual.

witch hazel
wet with rain
so cooling
to have
a choice

to reach
the edge of the well
at last
so thirsty for this water
underneath the ground

once in a while
a light falls through
a prism
soft rain clinking
the old townhouse roof

walking home
from the river
an empty shell
I sit and write
how it quickens the pulse

a crow
fails to swallow
something with feathers...
my permission
to fuck things up

a mesh
of dreams and wake
we breathe
onto each other
child and mother

in paler moonlight
a fox locks eyes with me
any moment now
we'll fall apart
—but this

I never tire of
looking at them—
the mountains
that blur
into mountains

the unpaved path ends
at the mountain's foot
all by myself
I turn to look at the woods
one last time

ACKNOWLEDGEMENTS

"we are the sum of our parts"

Failed Haiku, Volume 8, Issue 92
(part of the sequence "Eclipsed")

Cutouts (p. 1, 17, 29, 43)

Stardust by Neil Gaiman
The Sky Is Everywhere by Jandy Nelson
Kafka On The Shore by Haruki Murakami

Illustrations

Potato printing
Ink drawings on paper & collages
Digital drawing

by Kati Mohr

ABOUT THE AUTHOR

Kati Mohr, born in 1976, is a German disabled intuitive artist and poet, known online as pi & anne. She lives in Nuremberg with her family and two rabbits. Her aim is to explore the filters we humans use, because how we see things often says more about us than about the things themselves.

She is still busy creating a collage of her own life that makes sense to her.

Her poems have appeared in a number of journals, e.g. Kingfisher Journal, The Haibun Journal, Whiptail Journal, The Pan Haiku Review, MacQueen's Quinterly. She came second in the Marlene Mountain Memorial Contest 2023, organised by FemkuMag.

piandannes.wordpress.com
linktr.ee/pi.and.anne